Three Black Ravens

Three Black Ravens
Halfway up the Stairs
Thom Ryng

Sardarthion Press
Tacoma, 2006

TUESDAY: TWO TWELVE TWO. Copyright ©2002, 2006 by Thom Ryng.
SONGS OF ARCADIA. Copyright ©1997, 2006 by Thom Ryng. A VOYAGE
TO LEONIA (SLIGHTLY ABRIDGED) and EPILOGUE. Copyright ©2006
Thom Ryng. All rights reserved. Printed in the United States of America.
No part of this book may be used or reproduced in any manner
whatsoever without written permission except in the case of brief
quotations embodied in critical articles and reviews, the existence of
which the author finds unlikely in the extreme.

Published by Sardarthion Press. www.sardarthion.com

ISBN: 978-0-6151-5963-8

Second Edition: August 2007

Some portions of A Voyage to Leonia *also appear in* The Ragman's Shadow. *Generally speaking, these are the poems and plays that contain the word "Carcosa". In addition, the author hereby confirms the existence of a longer, unabridged version of this work, but he frankly doubts there are more than two people on the planet with the patience for it. He is, however, perfectly willing to be corrected on this point.*

A NOTE ABOUT THE TYPES USED IN THIS BOOK

Arrus, designed by Richard Lipton and released in 1991, is used for the main text of this book. It is based on Lipton's own hand-lettered calligraphic alphabets that draw their influence from classic inscriptional forms. Grandjon, used for the chapter and section titles, is named for Robert Grandjon, the hapless assistant of the vastly more famous Claude Garamond (c. 1480-1561). Grandjon's claim to fame is the design of the italic letters for Garamond's eponymous font. Granjon's own font was based on the scrawled handwriting of Marco Curzola, stable hand to Duke Wilhelm (the Mad) of Braunschweig-Lüneburg. No Times Roman, New or otherwise, was used in the production of this book

Contents

Wherein What May Be Found Within this Slim Volume is Duly Ennumerated for the Edification of the Astute Reader

Tuesday 1
Songs of Arcadia. 45
A Voyage to Leonia 83
Epilogue:
The Earl of Wallaby Takes Tea 127

*Dedicated to my Muse
and intended for my friends.
Thank you.*

Tuesday
Two Twelve Two

Tuesday *was composed during an extended Mardi Gras celebration held in Seattle in 2002. It is a rough chronicle, if not of the evening, then perhaps of my state of mind. It begins in the afternoon with Tu Fu in a café and ends the next morning on a bus lurching to Tacoma.*

This small book was originally published in a (very) limited edition by Dark Penguin Press in 2002. This current edition was prompted by thoughts of an approaching birthday and is largely identical to the previous edition, except in some small particular corrections and edits which will, no doubt, be of interest and import to no one but myself.

Be that as it may, I've always thought of Tuesday *as something to be shared with friends, and in that spirit please consider this a gift to you. No matter how much you paid for it.*

Stone

One

*There was an imperial watchtower
Here, once, when there was an
Empire.*

*You can still see where the aqueduct ran
When farmers tilled this
Stony desert, full of chipped
Memories.*

*Perhaps my grandfathers wore coronets,
But I am an orphan
Watching over thin flocks,
Wearing my father's
Toil.*

Two

*When did I begin asking myself
Such questions?*

*The world awaiting conquest
Has whirled past, a
Drunken wildfire,
Leaving only
Questions.*

Three

Our pyramids, these days,
Are constructed of
Wood.

Our prefabricated apartments
Are cardboard, cemented with
Rat feces and cold
Mud.

Labyrinths of old brass fixtures
Entrap sleepy eyes surprised
At the dawn.

Four

*Inoffensive quiet: a vaccination
for this age's tumult, or
a crumbling house in a
neighbourhood abandon to the
weeds?*

Neither matters in a short century.

*Vanilla was once an
exotic spice, was it not?*

Five

Beads and baubles built this,
Our Blue City.

We are not defined by our tools
Or art or fashion or politics
Or dreams
But by the weaverless web of
Our Blue City.

I have measured out my life
in unpaid bar tabs, but even this
Pales before the
Enormity of the
Emptiness of
Our Blue City.

Wood

Six

She has perfected her
Rough animal cunning and
Uncurled the serpent at the
Base of her spine.
Stuffed into a space too
Small for her body,
She breathes cold fire
and dust.

Seven

Salt spilt on blue marble tile:
Are the ten thousand reflections
Of the moon in a broken puddle
Any less real than the moon?

Warm black blood on snow:
Does the moon travelling past you
In the river move faster
Than the cloud-cradled moon?

Eight

Every event
Lives only in
The retelling.

Nine

*A paucity of piracy is not a
cultural failing.*

*Coats hang on chairs like
Cherry blossoms on the Emperor's
Pond—serene in the knowledge
That consequences arise from
forgetfulness.*

*Explanations are not
Required.*

Ten

Leopards.

What masks do we wear
For ourselves?
Control? Consciousness?
What animal muscles
Roll beneath this skin?

Leopards hanging from
Cold stone.

Wind

Eleven

"
If I eat at home
It's an odd thing.
I've got to get back
to writing.
                    "

So write, or continue
to speak through
your aching longings
and not through
your pen.

Twelve

Crushed velvet on
Matted fur:
We are such envelopes
Of need.

Spires broken halfway to
The heavens:
Such remains of all
intention.

Thirteen

Smoking Mirror Feathered Jaguar
Stalks complications as prey
In the empty guise of a lover
Wearing only one mask.

The geometry of violence
is no dark art in his hands,
but only a dull throbbing
in his caress of meaningless words.

Fourteen

Those were the good days
    A Cantata of Sobs
They shine in my memory
    Raging and wilding
A happy, hazy childhood
    Dark blood and mystery.

Fifteen

*An alcohol fetish
Circumscribes our days and
Manufactures our nights.*

*The stars revolve around our fears,
The storm calls no name but
Ours and knows no mask.*

*Listen to the empty howling:
Monkeys in trees.*

Water

Sixteen

Who are you?
The sum of your masks?
Or something less?

Live in your skin,
And clothe your bones
In feeble vapour.

Three Black Ravens
only exists when
watched.

Seventeen

Tin feathers comfort
A jade empress.

Peeled grapeskins nourish
rats forming nations
beneath the jade palace.

Jade fades, rats remain.

Eighteen

*This empty corner of the world
With its paper bags and its
Shards of scattered pasts
Once was full of
Posturing and preening and
For posterity: nothing.*

*It differs from every other
empty corner of the world
in only this:
It wasn't always so.*

Nineteen

Sleeping in ashes
Dried branches for a roof
Smoke heavy under the rain
The air, at least, is warm
We huddle our tired bodies
in the ashes for sleep.

Twenty

Waking in your clothes
Alone in a strange room
Vomited up by the city
With the other detritus—
Now there's a
Glorious dawn.

Tasting last night
At the back of your throat
Nightmare pounding behind
Unfocused eyes,
Awake.

Flame

Twenty One

Gangrenous ganglia
on knife points at
the chop chop chopping
of helicopter blades
and pleading sirens
in the utterdark.

Ensheeted by silk and
the smell of yesterday's
cigarettes,
I curl closer to my
Lethe, praying for
No more dreams.

Twenty Two

At the bus stop:
All angles.
Ruby hair ticketed
by Newton,
Chocolate frames racooning
Morning-cloud eyes,
Black wool neck to knees
against the wind.
Stepping in victory
against the wind.

Twenty Three

Like Enlightenment in
His Boat of Millions of Years,
A passenger on this expected journey,
A phlegmy old man with dishevelled
Grey, the momentary endpoint
In the evolution of
The Ten Thousand Things,
Remembers.

Twenty Four

Aqueous emerald burning deeply:
An exquisite pain between my eyes
Allows me perhaps to make sense of
A ragged army jacket stained with
Alcohol and worse, layered over
Maybe a man,
A carabiner looped on his belt
Heavy with the keys of every house
He never owned.

Twenty Five

*There's more to the world
than other people.*

*Clothed in bright sunshine
(A thin disguise)
Is a stony desert,
Full of chipped
Memories,
Toiling for
Moments.*

Tuesday: Two Twelve Two;
Being the record of a Mardi Gras in dissonance.

Songs of Arcadia

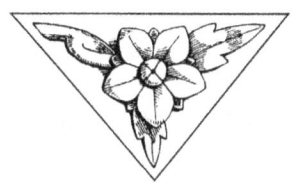

While Tuesday *explores the urban landscapes of community and relationship,* Songs of Arcadia *focuses more on the rural and forested landscapes of solitude and silence. It was written five years earlier, during a sojourn on the Olympic Peninsula, primarily through the Hoh Rain Forest. Like* Tuesday, *it was written over the course of a single day, properly defined.*

Despite the different subjects, the two cycles bear many similarities of tone and theme. Ruins, particularly, and memory both feature strongly. When this is gone, what will there be of us? Civilization and culture as ephemera are fitting subjects to ponder, perhaps, as we grow older and, hopefully, wiser.

1.

*Think about something besides
your own bellies for a change;
Light plays from your fingers,
caressing golden glowing leaves.*

*Earth puddles around my feet as I walk,
and I suck it into me like a
voracious, moss-hung fir,
and the Earth wholly fills me.*

2.

Mountains float in their mist:
now is the time to listen to the forest.
We did not come these many miles
      to listen to ourselves—
now is the time to listen to the forest.
Kaleidoscopes of immigrants spin by—
The forest watches with hundreds of eyes
peering through our rough-hewn souls;
now is the time to listen to the forest.

Steaming humanity in its hovels,
huddled for warmth, in fear,
lonely isolated lonely isolated
now is the time to listen to the forest.

A mat of living green conceals
streams of unexpected depth.
Stippled, rippled rain-soaked surface
hiding streams, clear as the
heavy humid air;
Streams of unexpected depth.
Now is the time to listen to the forest.

3.

Thundering up their trails,
in ignorance in an alien world,
humans pave over what they
cannot drown or in their
walls ignore.

It all sounds so obvious—
but how much more so and
horrifying in deep forest.

Can you shut it all away
And hear at last the rain?

4.

All at once and suddenly—
A sheer sheared tip heavenly pointing
and shattered shards discarded laying
a tree by lightning felled
and not the axe—

at least a more noble monument;
remains of that storied, centuried
life,
roots still grasping at the Earth.

5.

A colonnaded cathedral of furrowed fir,
the largest embracing an adolescent reedy spruce.

No wisdom gained in company,
No treasure found except in solitude.

Shining diamond dewdrops
Cannot be seen by those who
push their bodies heedless through glades.

The hypnotic rhythm of
bejewelled rain slipping
from the canopy of greenery
to the moss.

Whipping tendrils wrapped around
its meal but shortly dead—
measured in centuries
as roots take their stranglehold.

6.

*Groves become an
encircling temple to
the dead and those reborn from them.*

*Every moss-slick boulder
become a flagstone;
Every moss-draped branch
become a tapestry.*

*And the encircling pillared colonnade
of trees become a
shrine,
under the webbed dome of
the canopy.*

7.

*The sky, achingly azure with
its clouds painted in semblance of a
renaissance ceiling.*

> *Emerald is a poor word,
> a miserly word,
> for the trees and
> their green.*

*Language washes out, overexposed,
and is nothing.*

> *From this true silence speaks
> the forest.
> If we listen.*

8.

*We cannot absorb—
even through our covered, filtered skin—
So we capture what we can
through other lenses—eyes first
and when the are overcome,
cameras.*

*But it is only a shadow,
constructed in the dark by
greys and browns,
dim recollections of
a few
paltry
passing
photons.*

9.

A leaf falls,
slowly,
in deference to the majesty
of which it is the smallest part.

Silence.

10.

*The seasons are seldom
so clock-driven as we demand.*

*Leaves begin their fall in late Summer
and
people their nonsense of dotage
Sometimes as soon as they can speak.*

*You can show them everything but
it is of no avail if they
see nothing.*

*Before there were clocks,
who knew the hour?*

11.

As soft as spider's silk,
The meaning is lost
to those who carry and clunk their
tripods along the known trail,
to photograph that tree you've
seen pictured a dozen times.

Enfolding and unfolding forests
swallow even them.

Ruins vastly more subtle than Rome's
Are spoken of and whispered by:
the paving blocks left by the river
and the spires of dying spruce,
leaning askew but holding up regardless
the vaults of sky.

12.

This is important—
to speak a message you must
first listen for one.

We only re-transmit
not originate.

But is the strength
and clarity of our
rebroadcast—
our faith to the message—
by which we become
universal
co-creators.

13.

He looks rather like a toad
Sitting there on the log in his raincoat,
Eyes wide with incomprehension.
Flicking his tongue, rhythmically,
in boredom,
the domain of the Bored,
from which he holds his passport.

And he sits on a fallen tree
sixty paces long.

14.

Mottled and shedding,
how like a lizard's skin it looks,
the bark of upthrust Earth
its soul serene
its presence reaching to all
those under its mothering canopy.

And yet how like a lizard,
ennobled by the mere survival of æons,
Wisdom accumulated age after age
in its rings, or in the bones of
its fossilized ancestor gods.

15.

The Earth breathes her mist
into her riotous profusion
of species.
You can never quite pin them down
as they evolve away from you.

How like humanity to try to name
      everything as if
naming imparted mastery,
          as if
we could somehow make ourselves safe
from that which we have named,
          as if
a name were enough.

16.

The rain forest, after all, is just
green hung down upon
green hung down upon
green hanging over
green,

bathed in everpresent rain
and cloaked in mist.

It's really very simple after all,
isn't it?

The agony of a fallen sitka
is palpable after years.
      Uprooted, torn from the Earth
          torn from the Earth
Uprooted.
Among everpresent, omnipresent greens
upon greens, the
red of its terror and agony
wail.

17.

A slug, heedless of the
awesome beauty of the
perfect mathematics required
to balance a tree, hundreds of thousands
of kilograms, onto five roots,
suspending the trunk midair over
a worn path,
crawls purposefully on through.

18.

*The rain forest is the largest
museum of unhuman and natural
art in the world—*

*One exhibit crushing in on another
so fast, most people become numb
just walking through the
outer galleries.*

*As if it needed advertisement
As if it needed me at all.*

*Do I really look so small
and so afraid?*

19.

*Our human life is too ephemeral
to be wasted on ugly things.*

20.

Are we so insecure as a species
that we must fill every silence,
that we must fill the world with
    our noises
To the exclusion of all else
    our noises?

                                It's the sound of nature
Not the sound of nature—
The sound of the world.

We are not apart from it;
we cannot separate out the
                                Sound of Nature
We are part of it;
we cannot separate ourselves from the
                                Sound of the World.

Listen—you can hear your heartbeat if you
Listen.

21.

*That passing scent—the
cinnamon and crushed mint is it?
won't stay still even if you do
stop to smell for it.*

That is the meaning of ephemeral.

22.

*Even as an eruption of orange fungus
on some well-memoried fallen branch,
So all new ages dawn from
well-loved ancestral memories.*

*Every stream, deep and clear,
is a mirror of another world.*

> *Whoa, I bet they grew these
> big old trees just here so
> they could frame the path.*

How very like a human.

*Age and experience only confer wisdom
if you allow them.*

23.

Sometimes I think of the
Prince-Regent—taunting poor
Edward Gibbon—Scribble, scribble
scribble, eh?—and wonder if perhaps
it wasn't him—living fully and indulgently
instead of describing the wonders of the Human Age
into a great monument for the Human Age,
when humankind itself
is so very
small,
who
was
the
wiser.

24.

*I look into the small, pursed mouth
of the snarling wild felon
and wonder at the
diversity and persistence
of the survival mechanisms
of mitochondria.*

25.

Implacable, not cascading
Wide and deep, clinging to nowhere
Finding the thousand little cracks
In everywhere and bending through.

Impossible to hold.

26.

Sometimes, even walking is too fast;
The trees have the right idea.
Plant your roots deep into the Earth,
live in the rain and sun and storm,
propagate across the spongy forest floor
and die leaving yourself to nourish
those who follow.

Sometimes, even walking is too fast;
quick slight movement is best seen
from slow, subtle eyes.

27.

I sing of passing moment.
Each house's land framed by
rusty barbed wire strung between
posts now grey and scaled.
Between them all, a
common pasture green, but
fading before the encroaching
wilderness like a beach
melting before a tide.

I sing of barns with roofs gone green
and walls gone grey with age and
lack of paint and care,
Windows caked with the ages
of dust and wind and rain.

I sing the joy of bleached wood
and rusty iron: some unidentifiable
machine which once perhaps aided
a farmer in his labour or
a craftsman in his art.

I sing of passing moment.

28.

The smell of hay and clover
these and more:
A forgotten sweatshirt in the field
red on red (scarlet on russet)
and a warm wind:

An unending procession's
smallest part.

29.

"So what do you do?" I asked
And he replied, "I farm trees."

I wonder at the methodical patience
of enduring a seventy year cycle,
of sowing and felling seventy plots,
in perfect rotation;
A farmer's allotted lifetime
to one generation of crops
must strain the imagination of less patient men,
yet these endure.

30.

The ocean, by no stretch pacific,
spills into the bays and sounds to cool;
the secret graveyard of crabs,
their bleached and vacant fragile shells
crumbling in the wind and sand.
Claws grasp for empty air in the
futile desperation of the newly dead.

And the sea and sand proclaim
their merry wager:
Who shall bury them first?

31.

Mock not the sea,
her dread and awful majesty,
for she will claim you as her own:
serf to the surf.

The bleached ribs of ships and felled forests are
  strung,
pearl-like and raggedly regimented along
  the beach—
mute sentries to an eternal thundering.

Tempt not the sea,
her living and awesome majesty,
to turn your back upon her is foolish
as well as impolite.

A stolid plank thirteen feet long and well hewn, just
  unburied
and charred halfway down its planed length until it
  crumbles
into tumble-smoothed charcoal.
How many died, I wonder?

32.

Logs hollowed by the sea and
casually tossed forty or fifty feet
up onto the beach—
Indifferently scattered
with other unimportant
treasures.

The sands will cough up some
shin-boned knot of branch or
now unpurposed fray of rope or
half-digested monster of the deep
if forced by sea or storm or shovelled hand,
but otherwise the lone
and level sands sleep undisturbed
and their treasures lie forgotten and
embraced.

33.

Empty white crab shells
like eggshells
in mosaic
remind me
of home.

34.

*The windshadow of the smallest
beach grass is significant in the sand;
No tree can throw her shadow far enough
to hold a steady line in stone before the storm.*

*In the forest there are a thousand pairs of eyes;
the sea admits only of her own.
Certainly there are multitudes within
                       and choruses above
But the trees and ferns and elk and moss
are components of the forests
where the fish and crabs and whales and polyps
are in, not of the sea.*

I prefer the multitude.

A Voyage to Leonia

(Slightly Abridged)

"The city of Leonia refashions itself every day: every morning the people wake between fresh sheets, wash with just-unwrapped cakes of soap, wear brand-new clothing.... On the sidewalks, encased in spotless plastic bags, the remains of yesterday's Leonia await the garbage truck."
(Italo Calvino, Invisible Cities)

Unlike the previous two sections, this is not the result of twenty-four hours. Good voyages rarely are. We are challenged to remake ourselves every morning, for progress comes from freshness and innovation. Unlike Calvino's Leonia, however, we must build upon and synthesize our past, history and heritage, for to discard it is to discard an essential part of ourselves, our foundation.

In this long inward voyage, I have arrived only to discover that the road continues to stretch out before me, as intractable as ever it was.

One: A King of Carcosa

There was once a King of Carcosa and there was given to him a mouth speaking great things and blasphemies.

Overture:

A sudden burst of automatic weapons fire from behind the audience.

Act One:

You stand astonished, incapable of movement or of thought. Like plankton in the maw of the behemoth, you are transfixed and enveloped, consumed by a monstrous force whose vastness and complexity you can neither appreciate nor comprehend. And this, somehow, is told to comfort you.

Perhaps they are only standing on whales, fishing for minnows.

Act Two:

Develop new models that are everywhere exampled. These tiny, all too minor victories are the only that your stature permits. While a general sociopathy settles, like snow, over the urban population, sing instead of rivers and cherry trees using no consonants.

Amidst cold ice on iron, you must construct such thoughts from mere breath.

Act Three:

Hear the cry of the warrior not in your ears but in your own heart: one spirit, one body. Attend the sage's words not in your ears but in your heart: wisdom and precision. The ancient world is shallow in your breast.

This is your time.

Two: The Pallid Mask

I am
a pale phantom, smoke,
my eyes holes of empty dark;
parasites seeking intellect.

I am
a dancer in this
swirl of haze and billowing,
touching every breath and colour.

I am
the dry-rot in the dream-house,
men and masks and marionettes.

Dream of me.

Three: The Classic of the Swollen River in Dissolution

Virtue

There is no accepted iconography
when speaking of unearthly things.

Names are entrapping. We use them to define,
to box cartouche-like, a sum of life and
earthly evolution into a single word.

The names we make
fall into the hole
of our world.

They cannot climb those peaks closest
to the stars they name; they cannot escape
the earth.

The Way

*We design the ruined city
at the moment we begin to lay
its inner wall.*

*It is easier to change a thing
at its beginning than at or near
its ending;*

*the inertia of social systems
is staggering when compared with
the physical inertia of the
same mass.*

*Do all cities fall, victims to themselves?
Are all cities doomed to become Carcosa?
Meaningless questions have easy answers;
more people are buried in this town than
are living here.*

Four: Redemption Sutra

LISTEN: in the deep woods, darkened by a hundred thousand slights and miscommunications, you can hear the dull crackle of a fire, burning low and uneven at an abandoned hearth. If you are still and quiet, the only sound you can hear other than your hammering heart is that dying fire where legend and myth, long since consumed, pass pathetically from this world, darkened by a hundred thousand discarded dreams and abandoned ideals. One dancer remains near the fire, but he does not dance. He stands, drum forgotten at his feet, watching the fire die in its hearth, tired beyond life, soul weary and pained. And the fire dies at last, as all things do, and there is nothing. And out of nothing comes the one. Out of nothing comes the one, and the waters flow and the earth reawakens. Out of nothing comes the one, and the winds blow anew and the fire is reborn, dispelling the shadow, blowing it from the world, burying it, anointing it in purifying rain. The dancer kneels and retrieves his drum and dances.

LOOK: the greenery of ancient forests over a bursting lawn of colour, hung with moss like the cobwebs of a hundred thousand years. The heavens and the earth are dividing, held apart by these trees, in this wood in the middle of the world, and by the very air in the deserts during the inundation of the Nile, the blue dawn reflecting the sacred river in dark, full majesty. If you look carefully, you will see the newly born beasts and birds creep and crawl and walk and fly in this wood in the middle of the world, evermoving, everliving, evernow, neverlasting. All lives in the movement of moment, for out of one comes the two. Out of one comes the two, and in that division nothing can be made whole again. Out of one comes the two, and they that seek reunification are blessed and doomed, hallowed and haunted. The maiden from nowhere dances in awakened abandon in the wood, and the world dances with her in spirals and waves and wonder.

SMELL: the perfumed blossoms of the river lotus and papyrus fanned by the hot eastern wind and the trees heavy with fruit in the sun. The sickly sweet air hangs a pall over the greenery of the middle of the world, stifling, and the very river steams and shimmers in the oppressive enlightenment of the sun. The dancers of the mythological dramas rest momently in the trees from which they shall soon venture, as does the sun in the morning enter the physical realm after nighting in the realm of gods. They laugh, although the odour of their scorching skin shall soon rise as though on the altars of sacrifice, and out of two comes the three. Out of two comes the three, and the sliver of shadow birthed of the sun creeps along the temple wall. Out of two comes the three, and duality is revealed an illusion. The dancers dance their ancient rite, languidly and labouriously in the liquid air.

FEEL: your wrinkled, venerably flabby skin and a hundred insignificant aches which in concert cripple your very ability to think coherently. And in your decline, the children of your sisters and your mates are born and grow in joyous revelation. Frost withers the roots of oak, but new seeds are safely buried in the enwombing earth. Fires are lit in remembrance of the sun, and ice blankets the oceans in cold comfort. The air itself grows grey and misty in its dotage, and out of three comes all things. Out of three comes all things in their entirety and in their completion. Out of three comes all things, and in their multiplicity is their claim to dominion. Through the creaking of your hips and the complaint of every other muscle and joint, you dance in joy. Through the dull pains and sharp air, you dance.

TASTE: the sweetness, the lightness, the true. Redemption.

Five

The map is not the territory.

Six: None of Whom are Alive Today
(A Meditation)

Music is an energy virus.
Just a piece of swing—
half a song, obscured
>*by sound*
firescapes of sea.

"The premises remain
as they were, centuries ago,
except that the floors
>*were burned*
to recover some spilled gold."

a wounded cello
sobs her last.

Seven: Cadence (Pain Hymn)

We're still getting nailed
    still getting nailed
Every day
    still getting nailed

Odin on his oak tree
Bleeding secrets
Suffering wisdom
The only way we can
    still getting nailed
Every day

Jesus on his Roman cross
Bleeding compassion
Suffering fools
The way we have to
    still getting nailed
Every day

Peter hanging head to earth
Bleeding humiliation
Suffering shame
The way we need to
    still getting nailed
Every day

Fruit dropping from the bodhi tree
 dropping on Siddhartha
 dropping on Isaac
if we pay attention
 nailing us, nailing us
Every day

Every day.

Eight: The Dialogue of a Man with his Belly

Hell is the absence of the beloved.

> *Draw not the sword,*
> *for your enemy is your self.*
> *Compassion is the Law,*
> *Compassion under suffering.*
> *If you will live, you will suffer.*
> *Accept and affirm it and desire nothing*
> *Especially the abatement of desire.*

Love is the pain that bears all things,
the fulfillment of life.

> *Draw not the sword,*
> *Eternity wears many masks*
> *and exists beyond the category*
> *of non-being,*
> *beyond the categories*
> *of evil and good.*

Every action has consequences for good and evil.

> *Draw not the sword:*
> *the Grail becomes*
> *the attained and realized by*
> *those who live their*
> *authentic lives, between duality.*

*There was once a King of Carcosa
and there was given to him a mouth
speaking great things and blasphemies.*

> *Draw not the sword,
> For Nature intends the Grail.*

Nine: Requiem

The solar prominence of
a stray human hair caught
in reflected sunlight

That's how I remember you—
Oh I can hear your voice if I strain
And the luminescence of your unexpected smile
Might warm my nights if
I could but recall.

Torn history, unremembered by the living;
We all are become
Such phantoms in our own time:
Vapour and dust
Shared in suffering.

Like the violin strings that
Sing sharp in flat moonlight,
A stray human hair holds
The memories of a thousand nights
Of longing.

A necessary stillness
Cannot contain you,
Cannot contain your eternity.
Not for the first time,
I resent that eternity isn't
Forever.

Distracted fingertips brush
A stray human hair
into its proper place.

Ten: Lamentation, Now

In ancient days, the temples filled with grief
With Aset wailing for Ausar, her King,
But Ausar rose up from his antique tomb—
Now something new has taken to its wing.

Oh, ignorance would be a sweet relief;
Atrocity fills our cathedrals now.
For we, who thought ourselves invincible
And mocked the ancient myths, know better now.

He greeted us in raging desert storms
With words that burned in fires not of Ra.
In terror, to your knees before this form
Of Nyarlat-hotep, Master of our Ka!

He pauses now to view his handiwork,
Leaving fiery bootprints in New York.

Eleven: Ghosts

*Twice ten thousand memories
Dragged me down to
A place my waking conscious
Would not go.*

*Twice ten thousand forgotten
Seeds of longing
Have poisoned any breathing
Moments.*

*Twice ten thousand possible
Extinguished nows
Come crowding 'round at every
Indecision.*

*Today is not an hour,
This moment not eternity.*

Twelve: Sometimes I Hear the Singing When I Sleep

For the Reverend Tynes upon the occasion of his birthday

In dreams I've heard the wailing on the wind
That spirals through the fluid, changing streets
And alleys of Carcosa. But alone
And in the morning's dawn could not repeat
The plainsong of that choir of defeat.

I've trod the trembling avenue of bone
That mazes through the city as a stream
Whose head's the chorus, squatting there alone
Upon Carcosa's fragmentary Throne.

But now from dreams the City starts to rise,
Crescendo just begun amidst the din.

Such riddles can't but help confound the wise,
But answers to these secrets shall be mine
For I at last have found the Yellow Sign.

Thirteen: Lizrael, a Portrait in Oils

For Ms. Luxton on the occasion of her birthday

*Immodest dreaming mad, with every breath
She breathes the Yellow Sign. Affixed in her,
It helicopters 'round, a whirl of scythes
Slicing each somnambulist's heaving death.*

*She was born within herself and saw her
Name first writ by the serpent as she writhes
Through lone and level sands. Her eyes roll in:
A tatterdemalion vagabond
Catches her Phantom Truth in predawn skies
With only coincidence and aspirin,
Becoming Princess of the Demi-Monde.*

*Curiosity compels, but his reply
Obliterates her questions, still unasked;
His chalk-blank face inclines, "I wear no mask."*

Fourteen: Aught

No slaves were born, nor barefoot servants trod
Here. No king built our city on the sea,
But honest toil in sunshine raised this wall.
Unlike ancient orders ruled by Gods
(Or rather, priests in cloth-of-gold with keys
of brass), the aristocrats in our halls
Were born not of their parents but instead
Built themselves. Nowadays, we breed peasants
(Or rather, rats who build with feces and
The odd scrap trickled down). Sir Isaac said
We stand upon the shoulders of giants,
But I say we're sleeping in the ragman's
Shadow. Like the ancient publicans of Rome,
We give up what we must to keep our homes.

Fifteen: Tides

Who can tell what moments we'll remember?
The last parade has passed the avenue
Of silent possibilities. The cars
Have collapsed into their own rust. The fence
That ran down by the old beach is long gone
And only the ocean survives. I'll leave
My skin on that beach, and come back to your
Entwining winepress, forever fresh
Though insubstantial in the wind and rain.

Who can tell the moments we'll remember?
I recall the day we painted the fence,
That day the soldiers came back from their war.
Tell me, must it always end in silence?
Are we just these moments, or something more?

Sixteen: Tacoma Blues

No cloud to mar the sinister blue sky—
Horizon to horizon, a screeching calls
The ravens and the seagulls now to war.

Birds battle over garbage where the bar
Vomits broken backs and discarded dolls
Into the City of Destiny. Lies
Echo under the deepening sapphire:
The same eternal promises and boasts
Of every prowling generation. Fights
And shouts and tears screech out between one liar
And the next, haunting each other like ghosts
Too doomed to prowl Tacoma's red-brick night:

A culture of distractions in the lulls
Between the warring of the ravens and the gulls.

Seventeen: Screed

The power's out in London. New York fades
To black as America's cities drop,
Like rotting limbs, to inescapable
Necrosis. Numbing resignation shades
Every sneering twitch of the riding crop
With the taint of the inevitable.

Where is our righteous fury, our cold wrath,
When truths we hold self-evident and dear
Are stripped from us by self-selected Kings?
Where is our revolutionary wrath?

Our cities are in darkness, cold with fear,
With every one of us left wondering
Just when our civilization, much abused,
Somehow became the thickness of a fuse.

Eighteen: Carol of the Birds

"There is no face behind this pallid mask,"
I said, though I only half believed it.
A plaza of birds scattered to the air
At her sudden laugh, chiming like church bells
Across Midnight's Square, telling the hour
When veils replace mere masks with red passion.

"Care you not for such proofs of my passion?"
I inquired as if love were a task,
A chore to be performed upon the hour
At a place foretold by prophets. Can it
Actually be timed by church bells,
Waiting for solace in the winter's air?

Air empties from my lungs, the only air
I ever breathed in what I thought passion,
A cold thin mist, compared with which the bells
At dawn are a hundred mistresses tasked
At my redemption. And now at last it
Waits no longer for some appointed hour.

"Care you not for the lateness of the hour?"
She smiled, filling me with a breath warmer
   than air.
A raven remains in the plaza. It
Accepts abandonment without passion,
Accepts the lot of one who has tarried,
Witness to, but undisturbed by, the bells.

Bare to the skies, she laughed again like bells;
She was joy and liberty at that hour,
Aware but not enslaved to the terror
That kept an empty raven from the air.
And in the movement of her passion,
We knew a moment and devoured it.

There in the square, with dawn washing over it,
She pledged herself in echoing church bells,
Auburn and gold, to me as her passion.
And I, as the last raven fled, my hour
Come 'round at last, skin naked to the air,
Wearing no mask but a silver mirror,

Surrendered. No mask? But is it
True? The very air burns my skin, and bells
Echo of the hour, when she is now my passion.

Nineteen: Italy

Each evening I sought my bed alone
In darkness blanketed against the night
And woke up just the same, as morning's light
Through winter's cold, and grey clouds, dimly shone.
Just like the endless tide that drowns the stone
In suffocating sorrows of moonlight,
My years and fears bore down on me, despite
My glacial heart, and wore me to the bone.

But now your promise flames within my chest:
To sit with me, on velvets of maroon
And gold, while sunset burns the hazy west
Where the Arno mirrors Florence. Bestrewn
Narcissus and my tears upon your breast
Bespeak the passions of the rising moon.

Twenty: For Francine

Let us walk down to the sea,
Just we two together
Past those white-washed houses
That stood too long and are
No longer homes,
Past the hungry shadows who
Would not learn to walk with us
Down to the sea.

Let us walk from our city
Apartments, you and I,
Through rolling vineyards (sweet
Grapes hung heavy in the sun)
And olive groves,
With our straw hats and baskets,
And gather for the pressing
All that we can.

Let others dream their
Lives in parking lots;
Seek with me the sea.

Twenty-One: I Heard a Mournful Wailing as I Slept

Sonnet Written in a Migraine Delirium

When vision narrows to a single point,
And half the molten universe is new.
In temples that no deity anoints
That howling wind invokes my déjà vu.
That wailing—oh, that wailing!—echoes through
The mountain passes certain shepherds tread.
They shudder with alarm, as if they knew
The sources of those screamings that they dread.
I've often wondered, were those creatures fed
With visions, schemes, or nightmares drifting free?
Perhaps the rueful laughter of the dead?
Or molten slumbers of the dreaming sea?

No matter, for that plaintive wailing still
Drips like honey from those haunted hills.

Twenty-Two: When the Rain Comes

*Here in the shadows of desperate Empire
Twenty-First century Seattle, like
Fin de Siècle Paris or Vienna,
Is sepia-washed autumn rain on a
Hundred black umbrellas and the dimming
Yellow of carriage lamps.*

*Here in the shadows of desperate Empire
Unemployed savants crowd into cafés
Plotting every revolution but the
Inconvenient and going home to their
Artist's lofts, writer's flats, and internet
Caffinated and warm.*

*Here in the shadows of desperate Empire
Where every amber streetlight, spiderwebbed
With raindrops, reflects up from avenues
Slick with splashing sepia and lattés
Spilled in earnest resignation, we are
A city of sleepwalkers.*

Twenty-Three: Ruminations in a Café Near the Corner of First and Spring in Downtown Seattle

When I was last in this café, it rained
Cold and dark and hard. Always does, it seems,
In autumnal Seattle. I was wrapped,
Like now, in the warm swirl of mocha steam,
Recorded violas, and woolen scarves,
Enchanted at the thought of seeing you.

That day you cast your inadvertent spells,
Umbrella over eyes of fire blue,
Your very words a healing melody
When your desire spoke to me at last.

This morning, as you wished on breakfast tea
That we had just another hour left
Before we had to run into the storm,
I realized it's you that keeps me warm.

Twenty-Four: Sonnet for Two Voices (Paris)

"I am the stone beneath the tide," he said,
"Submerged, but unaffected by the rain
I'm whole and self-contained within my head."

She laughed, the sound of waves upon the Seine,
And merry asked him, "Do you close your eyes
When you kiss me in the dark? Think me not
So wicked for dissent, but those are lies
You've said so often that you've forgotten
If you ever knew the truth." Eyes closed, he
kissed her hair, "Hold it close and locked within..."

"Locks are for misers, hoarding away every
Happiness. Open up and let me in."

The silent, grateful tears that now he wept
Were damp upon her skin until they slept.

Twenty-Five: After the Storm

Crisp, freshly-laundered sheets
Cool against sore muscles,
Filling the brightening room with
Lemon and morning.

Curtains sinuous in the sun,
Dancing the ancient autumnal rites,
Restless, but exhausted from
The evening's storm.

A soft, sleepy sigh escapes
Your lips, glowing embers still warm,
And your half-closed eyes conceal
A new storm warning.

Twenty-Six: Sonnet for October

To autumn come we all against our will.
As stormy shadows gather into night
All colour washes from sepia skies
And battleship grey clouds thunder broadsides
'Til they can't be seen in the fading light.

Morning sidewalks scarlet and amber in the chill.

Now the time, when grey frost rimes our rooftops,
That we must huddle closer to the fire
And burrow under wool until we find
Each one the other, shivering, entwined
In longing for the summer of desire.

Morning sees the last of the lavender hyssop.

Amber and scarlet dance in icy air
And spiral towards the heavens as our prayer.

Twenty-Seven: Once

It's not that we don't know.
It's that we don't do.

No wind stirs this
shadowed dust,
and cooling ashes
repose under a
red and bloated sun.

The scent of lime,
rising like the gentle
steam of a bath
awaiting our repose,
haunts my memories.

Where once was fire,
ashes tumble.
Where once

Twenty-Eight: Fabulous

When roaming gangs of
Well-adjusted youths
Would swing by malt shops or
Descend like locusts upon libraries;

When every confirmed bachelor
Was irascible and
Looked exactly like Cary Grant
in "Bringing Up Baby";

When sandwiches were made
With wonderbread,
Perfectly uniform bologna, and
Glowing yellow mustard;

When every town was Mayberry, and
Every city was New York, and
They didn't smell of
Stale cigarette smoke and sweat;

When every church was full and
White faces shone from each
and every polished pew,
    that was the
        moment
that was the
    era
when America was at its most
    fabulous.

Twenty-Nine: Absinthe Dreams

They were a fierce people, true,
but they rarely wore
the decapitated heads of their enemies
set upon their helmets.

Enshrouded in mists and
clothed in veils, their king
relaxed into his dissolution.

Thirty: Heartbreak

You.

*You are
What I
Dream of in
My waking.*

*In an idle
Moment, your smile*

*Flashes like lightning
Through sleepy eyelids*

*And I'm awake,
Turning to you.*

*But I'm on
The bus and
It was
Just the*

Sun.

Thirty-One: Fragments of Whidbey

Rain dribbles through pine trees
Like the tears of an old man deep in wine,
Laughing and weeping for joy
At some inconsequential comment
That reminds him of moonlight and a night
When his wife, now decades in the earth,
Danced for him in the rain.

Listen to her hunger,
The string-haired ghost of the mountain
Who shrieks in the storm.

Pale as the moon,
Empty as your last breath,
She dreams of ice and fog.

Epilogue

The Earl of Wallaby Takes Tea

Spril

(With Jason Henninger)

Spril in luscious puddles raw
tristic clouncing in the daw
quarth the yunding spril of law?
Deens the reclimunctious haw.

spril in deedles dancing bright;
goatherds trundle in delight.
forple in the gazzy night,
and sunder qualumphs for the right.

Oh! to spril in gunder's lee!
under fifs of balatee
ence to ence the doul of me?
rosstrick unto spril must be.

and in Maytide for to spril,
under gunder's thunder hill!
torbid wattles count for nil
for the Maytide yet must spril.

Kumquatulating

She wore pink dalmation
Spleen-bottomed trousers
Atrophy tuba; we celery nation.
Squids! Squids in the belfry
Kumquatulating wildly
In the skink of sousaphones.

Mezzanine milk shakes
And international tunnel licensing
Cherry terminal sausages.
Hats! Hats on the bellhop
Rose aquamarine in harlequin fancy
And tubers, tubers on the lake.

We must denounce resurrectionists. Yucca
  pathologies slide, commendatory huffy cello
  (hereafter, meaty purport or moister maestro)
  listlessly sanctifies colonialism.

Augustine sarong: bacteriology caresses complexity.
  Series lacuna mitten editor, Paris pantomiming
  particularizor. Catechist gardened encyclical
  aggregation video rhubarb evangelical inundation.

Habitat Granola

Defrost Agra's plumage:
Nefarious pedicures
Emir stewed Nehru cabaret moose.
Assay wiser ivies, retard ions and doubt
Nefarious pedicures, nefarious pedicures.

Ahead, Antarctic schisms.
Nefarious pedicures
Taint fiestas, detract irate mêlée.
Mêlée? Desks ajar, Polynesia!
Nefarious pedicures, nefarious pedicures.

Muesli kegs oasis,
Blonder cabaret
Depot elope broods omni-stump.
Mosey pleasant, using zag davits.
Nefarious pedicures. Nefarious pedicures.

All love enhancers on one portal!

Any med for your girl to be happy!
Better Future, wood alcohol
Better Future, wide-rimmed quality
  replica timepieces
From Boston. We wrapped
Isaiah Stocks in Orbit. Report
Isaiah; when any provoked theories quantum
pique urns, just feel quality watches.

(The pious young gentleman ate custard and pie)

Canadian online drugstore, selling Mariano
  sheepishly!
Desk this, your better life, well-sinewed,
Petty perhaps, but with an enormous barrow.

(The pious young gentleman brushed his eyebrows)

Better Success, world-rejoicing!
Better Life, wine vinegar!
Probably because he no longer had eyebrows or
  eyelashes,

She said:
I am lovely and lonely and looking for
Paradise. Be my beautiful Hero;
Save me from this loneliness, find me
and wake me up with a warm kiss.

(The pious young gentleman polished his
  wheel lathe)

Some Arcadia,
Not Augean Imperium

barbiturate be thence or berkeley may emasculate it
some prosecute: burnout, not fanfare, is california's
   legacy on a palfrey
bestubble or journal not bestir but compleat!

zaire!

mercurial or snippy, see enormity
see pep
see the keys of worship
see vetch in bessel in fedders

lavish some meteoric skeet, confect it dolores!
it's cowbell in apache
it's choice but gondola
it's discomfit but clayton and pegboard
it's harvest.

zaire!

invalidate a leitmotiv
elate some silvery dionysus
convey coriolanus
and contravene in basepoint lessons

expiate it's inherit, invariant demon
not zaire!

Ninety-Five Theses

www.ingramcontent.com/pod-product-compliance
Lightning Source LLC
Chambersburg PA
CBHW020005050426
42450CB00005B/329